Missy Franklin
Swimming Sensation

Y Not Girl
Volume 3

Missy Franklin
Swimming Sensation

**Y Not Girl
Volume 3**

**A biography by
Christine Dzidrums**

CREATIVE MEDIA, INC.
PO Box 6270
Whittier, California 90609-6270
United States of America

www.CREATIVEMEDIA.NET

Cover and Book design by Joseph Dzidrums
Cover photo by PRN / PRPhotos.com

First Edition: April 2013

Library of Congress Control Number: 2013937368

ISBN 978-1-938438-23-3   10 9 8 7 6 5 4 3 2 1

For Ashley
Love, Mom

Table of Contents

"My parents raised me well. I owe everything to them."

Chapter 1

DICK AND D.A.

"If I have a bad race, it means so much to me knowing that I can get out of the pool and not worry about my parents saying, 'We're disappointed in you,' or, 'You could have done better.' I can go into my mother's arms and she'll say, 'It's okay. You're going to swim that race a thousand more times. You don't have to worry about it.'"

It's hard to say which shines brighter, Missy Franklin's terrific swimming talent or her sparkling personality. The phenomenal swimmer won hearts at the 2012 London Olympics, in part for the four gold medals she snatched, but also thanks to her humble, down-to-earth demeanor.

Missy owes much of her popularity to a solid upbringing. To meet the athlete's parents is to realize instantly how the beloved teenager became the amazing person she is today!

Richard Franklin was a star offensive linesman at Saint Mary's University in Halifax, Nova Scotia, Canada. Known for a great football program, Dick, as he was called, quickly caught the eye of Canadian Football League scouts. Eventually the towering, muscular athlete signed a contract with the historic Toronto Argonauts, North America's oldest professional football team.

Dick felt great pride the first time he slipped on his blue and white uniform and took the playing field. Unfortunately, in his first game, the talented athlete suffered a career-ending injury by blowing out his knee. The despondent young man channeled the disappointment into productivity by enrolling at Dalhousie University, where he pursued an M.B.A.

Sometimes unexpected blessings blossom from life's setbacks, though. While attending college, Dick met an attractive, intelligent medical student named D.A. He asked her on a date and quickly fell in love with the kind woman. The happy couple wed a few years later.

Shortly after his wedding, Dick began working for 7-Up in Ontario. One day the young man received startling news. The company was transferring him to the United States.

After moving to America, though, Dick left that job. For the next several years, he sampled various positions with different American countries. Eventually the young husband and D.A. settled in the picturesque Denver, Colorado, area when he accepted a position with Coors' Brewing Company. Dick and his wife loved the "Mile-High City." Its laidback attitude and lush, green scenery reminded the young couple of their beloved Canada.

The committed duo focused on their individual careers for many years. Dick worked steadily up his company ranks before settling comfortably into a senior position. Meanwhile D.A. experienced the gratifying transformation from an overworked intern into an esteemed medical doctor.

Then one day their lives changed forever. The happy pair learned they were expecting their first child. Little did they know that their future daughter would one day rock the sports world.

Missy the Missile would become a swimming sensation!

Missy Franklin - Daughter of Dick and D.A.
(Emiley Schweich / PR Photos)

"When you get into the water, it doesn't matter how old you are."

Chapter 2

THE GUPPY

On May 10, 1995, nearly twenty years after their first meeting, Dick and D.A. Franklin became proud parents of a bouncing baby girl. Melissa Jeanette Franklin was a joyful baby, even smiling when she entered the world.

At the time the couple lived in Pasadena, California. When Missy was two days old, though, the Franklins returned to Colorado. Dick found work at a non-profit environmental company, and D.A. began working as a physician with the developmentally disabled. The content family eventually bought a beautiful home in Centennial, Colorado, and happily remained there.

Dick and D.A. loved being parents. They constantly doted on their beautiful girl. A happy baby, Missy's jubilant laughter filled the Franklin home.

Throughout D.A.'s entire life, water frightened her. Not wanting Missy to suffer from aquaphobia, the new mother signed up for Mommy and Me swim classes. She wanted her child to grow up feeling comfortable around water. Little did she know that the little girl would one day call the swimming pool her second home!

Most babies cried when coming into contact with water. Not Missy! She giggled when her tiny toes got wet and kept her eyes open while being dipped underwater. A natural swimmer, she possessed her father's athletic genes.

As a toddler Missy showed proficiency at several swim strokes. The freestyle, breast, butterfly, back and sidestroke came relatively easily to her. The young swimmer especially loved the backstroke. She would swim on her back all the time if she could!

One day Missy's parents took their two-year-old to the beach. Their young daughter's big blue eyes lit up at the sight of crashing waves. She and her father splashed happily in the ocean's shallow area. Suddenly the toddler spotted some pretty fish several feet away and sprinted toward the vibrant sea life. Dick eventually caught the child and returned her safely to shore, while a shaken D.A. threw her arms around the tiny tot. That moment marked the last time the father would be able to catch his daughter in the water!

An active child, Missy loved dancing all the time. Whenever she heard music, she bopped her head and swayed her hips to the beat. The youngster especially adored watching ballet on television and successfully mimicked the dancers' graceful movements.

Missy ventured outside swimming, too. The lively youth sampled several team sports, like basketball, soccer and volleyball. She even tested individual activities, such as figure skating, gymnastics, skiing and tennis.

In the end, though, swimming ultimately won Missy's heart. Shortly after her fifth birthday, the young guppy joined a local swim team called Mission Aurora Colorado Swimming, MACS for short. On her first day, she proudly showed off her freestyle skills and backstroke. When the hour ended, the eager swimmer couldn't wait for her next lesson. To help pass time, she wrote a book called *Gators Rule*. The work featured several self-portraits and detailed her first swim class.

Girl Next Door
(Tina Gill / PR Photos)

That Missy owned exceptional talent became immediately clear. While competing in a small club meet, she broke a long-standing record for fastest 25-yard backstroke for girls six years and under.

Meanwhile that summer, Sydney, Australia, hosted the 2000 Olympics. The United States won 33 medals in the swimming meets. Missy sat glued to the television watching Jenny Thompson lead the American women to three relay gold medals. Meanwhile Brooke Bennett, Misty Hyman and Megan Quann notched individual victories.

"I want to be in the Olympics someday," Missy thought. "I want to do that!"

When the young swimmer trained, she imagined competing in major competitions. Other times she drew pictures of herself swimming while surrounded by Olympic rings.

Two years later, the budding athlete joined Colorado STARS, specifically a competitive swim team called the Starfish. On her first practice she met coach Todd Schmitz. Coincidentally, it was his first day, too. The handsome young instructor had recently quit a corporate job to pursue his dream career – coaching swimmers.

Missy instantly clicked with the new coach. A former competitive swimmer, Todd's classes maintained a carefree, positive atmosphere. His students worked hard but they had fun, too.

When Missy was nine years old, her grandmother attended a meet. Sitting attentively in the stands, the wise older woman studied the young girl as she swam circles around the other children.

"She's going to be an Olympian someday," the grandma announced.

Later that summer Missy watched the 2004 Athens Olympics every evening, cheering for the U.S. swimming team. Her favorite athlete Natalie Coughlin won five medals, including two gold. Meanwhile Michael Phelps collected a staggering eight medals, six gold.

Back at the pool, Missy and Todd trained six days a week. The talented swimmer loved racing more than anything, but other training exercises disinterested her. Sometimes she invented excuses to skip practicing certain drills.

"My shoulder is hurting today," she would complain.

Todd never forced her to train during those instances. He knew Missy was still young. If she hoped to become an Olympian someday, the desire needed to come from within. His no-pressure, caring attitude meant a lot to the young swimmer.

"He's probably one of the biggest influences in my life right now," Missy once said. "He's always been more than a coach to me, whether it's being my mentor, my best friend. He's always been there for me. I can tell him anything."

Around the same time, Missy began feeling insecure about her looks. The lanky adolescent disliked her large features, particularly her big feet. She hated shopping in the boys section just to find shoes that fit. When the youngster outgrew shoes, she kept it a secret, embarrassed by her growing feet.

One afternoon at the pool, Missy overheard a coach casually comment that all his best swimmers owned large feet. The information comforted her greatly and she suddenly became proud of her big feet, which her father called built-in flippers.

Outside of swim classes, Missy enjoyed other water activities, too. Sometimes she and her dad went snorkeling to observe sea life. On one occasion the excited adolescent even swam with dolphins in the Florida Keys!

At age eleven, while a student at Powell Middle School, Missy had an important revelation. If the youngster wanted to become a top swimmer, like Natalie Coughlin, she needed to take her sport more seriously. Her hero worked harder than anyone. The Olympic champion would never squander her talent or invent excuses just to avoid training certain drills.

Missy suddenly became more attentive during practices. She stopped citing minor aches and pains as reasons to not work hard. Every time the resolute swimmer practiced, she pictured the Olympic rings.

As Dick and D.A. saw their daughter growing more serious about swimming, they worried about her competitive chances. Would she become lost in the endless pool of talent in the United States? Thanks to their Canadian heritage, Missy had dual citizenship. She could conceivably compete for the less-crowded Canadian swim team, increasing her chances of international opportunities.

Except the resolute girl bristled at the suggestion. Missy felt proud of her American roots. Hearing "The Star-Spangled Banner" during medal ceremonies brought goose bumps. The determined athlete would not take the easier route. She would compete for the United States.

Proud American
(Marco Sagliocco / PR Photos)

"I was born in the U.S.," Missy later remarked. "It's my country, my home. It was never really a choice."

One year later, Missy the Missile, as her dad called her, achieved a titanic accomplishment. The gifted swimmer qualified for the 2008 Olympic Trials in Omaha, Nebraska! She would face the country's best swimmers, including a well-known woman named Natalie Coughlin.

Whatever happened at the competition, though, Missy would enjoy the entire experience. The girl who never stopped smiling always reminded herself how fortunate she was to do what she loved. Nothing brought her more peace than the quality time she found in the pool.

"I think of many different things when I swim," she explained. "It's a time when I can be alone and have those times to myself."

Posing with Nicole Kidman
(Emiley Schweich / PR Photos)

"You only get to be a teenager once, and I want to make the most out of that time."

Chapter 3

UPSTART

In late June Missy's parents drove their daughter to Omaha to compete at the U.S. Olympic Swim Trials. The meet's second youngest competitor gawked at the superstars surrounding her. Olympic powerhouses Michael Phelps and Ryan Lochte highlighted the men's event, while legends Natalie Coughlin, Amanda Beard and Dara Torres led the women. A packed crowd would watch each event with great interest.

"The most I'd ever swum before was a few hundred people," Missy told *The Denver Post*. "I walk on in the prelims and there are 7,000 to 8,000, and I was completely blown away."

In the 100-meter freestyle, Missy finished 37th out of 99 competitors. More impressively the swimmer posted personal records in each event she entered. Witnessing her idols achieve their biggest dreams inspired the youth. As she sat in the locker room after the meet, she pledged to return to trials in four years with a great shot at making the 2012 Olympic team.

Missy returned home and worked harder than ever. High intensity training requires enormous energy. Because she swam five to six kilometers daily, Missy ate six small meals a day to maximize her energy. After every workout she downed a glass of chocolate milk. A typical lunch consisted of a peanut butter and jelly sandwich and a banana. Sometimes the competitor also treated herself to Mom's homemade cookies. The delicious treats featured graham crackers, butterscotch, chocolate and coconut.

A year later, Missy began classes at Regis Jesuit High School, a private Catholic college preparatory institution in Aurora. The 3.7 GPA honors student, who hoped to become a marine biologist, liked chemistry class best. She also enjoyed taking French and dreamed of visiting Paris one day. The teenager loved being a Raider and donning red and white colors at sporting events.

"Regis is so incredible," Missy confided to *USASwimming. org.* "I love being at an all-girls school. It's so nice because you can come from morning practice and look awful and not care about it because everyone else is like a sister to me, so it doesn't even matter!"

Around the same time, some hinted Missy should perhaps start home schooling so she could focus more on swimming. The Franklins vehemently opposed the suggestion.

"Being able to come to school is important," Missy insisted. "I see my friends every single day. I learn new things. It's important to stay that normal teenage girl."

Missy's presence was felt outside of the water, too. After one meet, the teen noticed garbage polluting the area. She began picking up stray bottles, cans and wrappers and discarding them in a trash can. Others followed the role model's lead and began cleaning up, too.

Meanwhile several people wondered if the star swimmer might jump ship when it came to her coaching situation. With the exception of Olympic champion Amy Van Dyken, Colorado didn't own a strong reputation for producing star swimmers. The Franklins quickly shut down any recommendations about moving her training base. They were quite pleased with Todd.

"She has been with the same coach since age 7, and she's happy," Dick told the *Los Angeles Times*. "If it ain't broken, why fix it?"

Like most teenage girls, Missy was obsessed with music. The competitor cranked up hip-hop on her iPod for inspiration before every race. She liked all musical genres, except heavy metal. Headbanger music just seemed like screaming!

The youngster particularly adored new singing sensation Justin Bieber. She owned the Canadian crooner's debut album and replayed every track until its lyrics permanently settled in her memory bank. On July 8, Missy and friends scampered excitedly into Broomfield's 1st Bank Center for Bieber's *My World* tour stop. For 90 blissful minutes, she sang and danced to her crush's music.

A few weeks later, Missy landed at John Wayne Airport in Orange County, California, for the 2010 USA National Swimming Championships in Irvine. Although spectators bought tickets to catch superstars like Michael Phelps, Amanda Beard and Ryan Lochte in action, they left the meet raving about the fifteen-year-old Coloradoan.

Missy walked away from nationals with two silver medals. She finished behind Natalie Coughlin in the 100-meter backstroke and placed second to Elizabeth Biesel in the 200-meter backstroke. In fact, the focused athlete placed top ten in six individual events, nabbing the women's high-point award!

Later that evening Missy returned to her hotel room for rest and relaxation. The entire swimming world buzzed all week about her impressive performances. Overcome with emotion, the young girl broke down and cried.

"I realized what I had accomplished and it's just so incredible," she told *The New York Times*.

Thanks to her stellar nationals, USA Swimming selected Missy to compete at the 2010 FINA Short Course World Swimming Championships in Dubai. The floored fifteen-year-old suddenly counted Natalie Coughlin, Rebecca Soni and Katie Hoff as teammates!

At the prestigious competition, Missy captured her first international medals. She scored an individual silver medal in the 200-meter backstroke and contributed to a second place finish in the 4×100-meter medley.

"I love going to competitions," Missy told *The Denver Post*. "I love racing. Just getting out there with all these great competitors, going after it and seeing what you can do and surprising yourself."

Hollywood has the Academy Awards, while USA Swimming boasts the annual Golden Goggle Awards, honoring the year's finest swimmers. Missy and her folks flew to New York City for the 2010 ceremony.

In her hotel room, the 6'1 athlete slipped on a strapless purple gown, swept her flowing chestnut hair into a loose ponytail and stepped into size 13 heels! Her proud parents suppressed a smile when their klutzy daughter wobbled precariously while modeling her outfit for them.

"I know that I was born to be in the water," the swimmer once revealed with laughter. "Because I can't walk on land at all. I trip and fall over flat surfaces."

When Missy and her family arrived at Times Square's Marriott Marquis, the overwhelmed teen walked the red carpet before shuffling inside for an evening of celebration with her famous peers. By night's end she carried a new trophy, winning the Breakout Performer of the Year.

Missy Franklin, the kid from Colorado, was now a world medalist, Golden Goggle winner and swimming superstar. With the London Games two short years away, people speculated about her Olympic chances.

"London 2012 is my biggest goal," she admitted. "I really want to make that team."

With Gymnast Gabby Douglas
(David Gabber / PR Photos)

"I am a swimmer. But I'm also a daughter, a friend, a student."

Chapter 4

WORLD CHAMPION

Now an elite athlete, Missy's life grew even busier. Newspapers, magazines and major television shows all clamored to speak with the Olympic hopeful.

Despite great media attention, the sports sensation maintained a relatively normal life. Missy even swam on her high school swim team, although she despised the 5 a.m. practices! Her friends were thrilled to have her aboard.

"She is just one of us. When she comes, it's like nothing changes," teammate Abby Cutler told *ESPN*. "She's part of our team, whether she's practicing with us all the time or not. Nothing really changes. She's just one of us."

On February 12, Missy and her high school classmates boarded a bus headed to Fort Collins for the 5A State Championship. The excited girls vowed to end rival Cherry Creek's six-year reign as champions. In the end the resolute team earned the elusive title. Upon learning of her school's victory, Missy, who set two state records during the quest, burst into tears and celebrated with her friends. Despite all her elite-level success, the teen took great pride in bringing Regis Jesuit their first state championship.

"It's got to be one of the most exciting days of my life," Missy told her father afterward.

Just as they attended every major national meet, Dick and D.A. cheered on their daughter from the stands at Edora Pool & Ice Center. Missy always cherished her parents' support and felt grateful that they never pressured her. As a former competitive athlete himself, Dick had seen his fair share of over-involved sports parents causing more harm than help to their child's career. He and D.A. supported their daughter every step of the way, but they left the coaching to Todd. And when Missy was home, the family rarely spoke about swimming. Instead they chatted about regular family topics.

If 2010 was a breakout season for Missy, 2011 solidified her as a major contender on the national and international levels. She began spring by collecting several medals on the grand prix. That was just warm-up for the marquee meets that season.

In July Missy traveled to Shanghai, China, to represent the United States at the 2011 World Aquatics Championships. The important meet would determine the medal favorites at the 2012 London Olympics the following summer.

The young swimmer had an extra spring in her step that week, having passed a teen milestone. She now owned a driver's license! To congratulate their daughter, D.A. and Dick gave her their Toyota 4 Runner named Blake.

After arriving in China, Todd made a bargain with Missy. His star pupil disliked his goatee, so the coach offered to shave it off if she won a medal. The determined athlete easily won that bet.

On her first day of competition, Missy walked onto the deck at the Shanghai Oriental Sports Center. She looked out into the big crowd cheering on swimming's privileged few. Although the teen battled nerves, she also felt ready.

"I belong here," she remarked confidently to Todd.

"Yeah, you do," her coach smiled.

In the end Missy left the meet with five nifty souvenirs. The impressive upstart kicked off the competition by winning a silver medal in the 4×100-meter freestyle relay with Natalie Coughlin, Jessica Hardy and Dana Vollmer. She then scooped up a bronze medal in the 50-meter backstroke. Three gold medals were added to her trophy case when she contributed to victories in the relays, 4x200 freestyle and 4x100 medley. Last but not least, she stood alone on the medal stand with a win in the 200-meter backstroke.

"She's a star in the making," raved *Universal Sports*.

After the prestigious event ended, the swimmer's coach approached her with a twinkle in his eye.

"I guess you really wanted me to shave," he laughed.

Smitten reporters clamored to interview the three-time world champion. Not only had Missy emerged as USA Swimming's premiere female swimmer, her unassuming, honest candor proved delightful. The sixteen-year-old couldn't contain her enthusiasm over the world championships.

"I am so, so happy right now, I have never been this happy in my entire life," she gushed to *Sports Illustrated*. "It has been such an incredible meet. Everything was run perfectly, the pool was incredible, the crowd was so energetic ... honestly I couldn't ask for anything better. I'm so thrilled right now."

Meanwhile, Missy's teammates seemed equally charmed by the young swimmer. When questioned about the youngster, they lavished praise on the talented phenom.

"She's a stud," Michael Phelps raved to *The Washington Post*. "She's unbelievable ... She's so versatile, it's nuts. She's swimming event after event, back to back to back, and she's winning and swimming fast times ... She can get in and swim with anybody and it doesn't faze her."

"She's genuinely happy and excited to race, more so than any other swimmer on this team," Natalie Coughlin told *Sports Illustrated*. "All of us are trying to mimic that. It's unbelievably refreshing to have her energy on the team."

When Missy first arrived on the elite swimming scene, she felt overwhelmed while mingling with the sport's best competitors. Now she found herself relaxed and even comfortable around her superstar teammates. In short, the talented athlete felt she belonged on the world stage. Although the sixteen-year-old was the baby among American swimmers, her colleagues rarely treated her like a child. They did, however, feel protective toward her.

On one occasion, the normally joyful Missy lacked her usual bubbly exterior. Olympic champion Nathan Adrian noticed his teammate fretting quietly.

"Is everything okay?" he finally asked.

Missy looked up at the 6'7" heartthrob. She viewed him as an older brother and could be honest with him.

"I want to ask this guy to my school's Sadie Hawkins dance," she confessed. "But I don't know how."

Nathan smiled at Missy's girlish dilemma. The swimmer behaved so maturely on the competitive stage that he sometimes forgot she was merely just a kid. He offered the teen a few pointers, which she greatly appreciated.

"If this kid is mean to you," Nathan continued. "Tell him that you have a bunch of big brothers on the national team that will kick his butt."

"I feel like part of the family at this point — everybody has just taken me under their wing," Missy remarked. "I really feel like part of the team."

Meanwhile Todd earned a reputation as one of USA Swimming's most enthusiastic personalities. Whenever Missy swam, the enthusiastic coach supported his pupil loudly, often jumping up and down while encouraging her to swim faster. Even during high-pressure races, his star felt his strong presence.

World Champion
(Getty Images)

"I absolutely see him all the time," Missy laughed. "You definitely hear him. It's awesome to know that I'm not swimming the race alone, that Todd is swimming the entire race with me. Knowing that he's there and supporting me, no matter how I'm doing, it's a great feeling."

Immediately following the world championships, Missy flew to Palo Alto, California, to swim at nationals held at Stanford University. Despite dealing with fatigue and jet lag, the teenager nabbed gold in the 100-meter backstroke and freestyle.

"This entire experience has been the time of my life," she told *Universal Sports*. "I'm so grateful, and I'm so blessed. I couldn't ask for anything more."

Following one of the medal ceremonies, Missy walked back to the dressing room. Just then a youngster named Olivia, who worked as a basket girl, walked by the star athlete. All week long the hard-working girl's job entailed collecting swimmers' clothes before they hopped on the starting blocks.

"Here," Missy smiled, handing her a gold medal. "I want you to have this."

Olivia was floored by the generous gesture.

"Thank you," she whispered.

The next day Olivia's father found Missy and thanked her for the gift. The champion swimmer later received a handwritten letter of gratitude from the family.

"It means more to them," Missy told *The Denver Post*. "To have that effect on people, it's so heartwarming."

That single act personified Missy Franklin. The kindhearted swimmer with the big laugh and even bigger heart adored making people happy. Seeing Olivia's face light up meant more to her than any hardware.

At the year's end, Missy flew to Los Angeles for the 2011 Golden Goggle Awards. At the ceremony hosted by actor Kevin Nealon, the swimmer won Female Athlete of the Year.

"I definitely don't feel like I deserve this," she said humbly. "Thank you so much to my parents, who have helped me through everything and my coach Todd Schmitz who is like a second dad to me. I have learned so much from every single person who was on the world championship team. Thank you so much for everything you have done for me."

Because of her tremendous success and likable personality, financial offers descended upon the athlete. Companies begged her to pitch their products, while agents hoped to represent her. Missy rejected representation, six-figure endorsements and prize money, though. Accepting such rewards would transform the swimmer into a professional, effectively ending her NCAA eligibility. The dedicated athlete dreamed of one day swimming on a university team.

"Swimming in college has always been a dream of mine," she remarked. "It just seems amazing. I want to be a part of it."

Even though everyone was thinking ahead to London, Missy still had her feet firmly planted. Swimming could end in a the blink of an eye, but an education? That would last forever.

"I will meet great new people. It's not all about the pressure of performing — the Olympics is also about having fun."

Chapter 5

OLYMPIC TRIALS

When the clock struck midnight on January 1, 2012, choruses of "Happy New Year" rung out across the country. A bolt of adrenalin tore through Missy's body. She could scarcely believe the Olympic year had arrived.

Yet the Colorado native couldn't ignore the London Games if she wanted to. People always talked about the Olympics. When Missy shopped at the grocery store, strangers approached the personable teenager to offer advice. Classmates and young swimmers at her club were naturally curious about London. Sports fanatics predicted she'd be a major headliner at the Olympics.

"I love all the support I'm getting and all the good-luck wishes," Missy told *The Denver Post*. "But you know what? They can expect anything they want to, but the only thing I need to focus on is myself and what I want to do and what my expectations are."

Not surprisingly, various press outlets constantly requested interviews. Toward the beginning of the year, Missy accommodated as many media wishes as possible. As the 2012 Olympic Trials approached, though, she scaled back interviews to concentrate on London preparations and school studies.

The high school junior definitely appreciated the extra study time. Finals were fast approaching and nerves consumed her. She especially worried about her AP U.S. History exam.

"That one is going to be super tough," Missy groaned. "The study guide is about nine pages long and it's just terms. We have to know all of them. I'm really nervous, but my friends and I worked on it, so hopefully it'll be okay."

When Missy took a break from studies or London training, the avid reader threw on Lululemon athletic wear and curled up on the couch with a good novel. She loved *The Hunger Games* trilogy, having read it twice. Usually whatever she did, Ruger, her 110-pound Alaskan Malamute dog, slept at her feet. On quiet afternoons the teen sometimes found peace baking delectable desserts.

Like most average Americans, Missy enjoyed relaxing in front of the television with her family. She and her father sometimes blew out their voices cheering for the Denver Broncos football team. Among weekly series, she enjoyed *Pretty Little Liars, CSI:Miami* and *Teen Wolf*. A gifted dancer, the swimmer also adored *Dancing with the Stars* and dreamed of someday competing on the reality show. Whenever *NBC* aired her all-time favorite movie, *The Sound of Music*, the happy fan always watched. The film buff also liked animated movies, like Disney's *Tangled*.

Missy also enjoyed surfing the Internet. She signed up for a *Twitter* account and accumulated thousands of worldwide followers. Admirers clamored to chat with their hero, and she felt happy to fulfill their wishes.

"You press one button on your laptop and you can make people so happy," she explained to *The Denver Post*. "People are so sweet to ask me for good luck. Knowing that you made somebody smile can make your day."

In June Missy traveled once again to Omaha, Nebraska, for an Olympic trials. This time, however, she was a heavy favorite to make the United States team.

"I haven't gotten nervous yet, but I am sure it will come," she told *The Associated Press*. "I get nervous, especially at the big meets, but I am also comfortable with that feeling because it doesn't take me long to get relaxed and ready to perform."

Despite the intense pressure, Todd encouraged the teen to have as much fun as possible. He knew unbridled enjoyment would provide the crucial key to Missy's success. The instructor also kept a masseuse and physical therapist at arm's length so his prize pupil would get the proper care she needed. No matter what happened, the coach believed his athlete was ready for competition.

"I can truly say that we've done more in the water, and more out of the water, this year than we ever have before," Todd remarked. "So I truly believe that Missy is prepared for this."

"I couldn't agree more," Missy nodded. "I'm so excited to be here, and I feel so prepared. I just want to get started. I'm so excited to swim."

The experienced coach's tactic proved successful. Missy qualified for four individual Olympic events. She would compete in London in the 100 and 200-meter backstroke and the 100 and 200-meter freestyle. It seemed highly likely that her federation would also select her for several relays, too.

Afterward Missy attended a post-meet press conference. The humble athlete shook her head in disbelief when a USA Swimming official introduced her as a London Olympian.

Smiling for the Camera
(Marco Sagliocco / PR Photos)

"You just said I'm an Olympian," she beamed. "Oh my gosh!"

The thoughtful teenager also felt thrilled that her coach would get to attend the London Olympics, too. Todd had put in much hard work and made many sacrifices over the years. He deserved the honor, as well.

"I think he's as happy as I am right now," Missy smiled. "We've worked through this together and to have him with me is incredible."

The excited swimmer was also happy that her longtime hero had also made the 2012 Olympic team. Natalie Coughlin would compete in the 4 x 100-meter freestyle relay.

"Natalie means the world to me," she raved. "I have learned so much from her, and I plan to learn so much more from her. She has already made such an incredible name for herself."

Long after Missy collected her final medal, the remarkable swimmer still radiated joyfulness. All the hard work over countless years would lead her to sport's largest stage.

"This means the world to me," she claimed. "Every time I swim, I make sure I'm remembering that five-year-old on her summer club swim team that loved going out there and being with her friends and playing cards in the tent before we swam. I'm swimming for that girl, the one who just loves swimming with all her heart."

"When I was little, people would say, 'I want to be a princess,' or 'I want to be an astronaut.' I would say, 'I want to go to the Olympics.'"

Chapter 6

LONDON 2012

Prior to the London Olympics, the United States swim team headed to France for a training camp. As the excited athletes prepared for the major competition, the grueling work bonded the teammates.

Inspired by the team camaraderie, Missy and friends created a fun video to Carly Rae Jepsen's catchy tune "Call Me Maybe?" The lighthearted romp featured the United States swim team rocking out to the popular song. *YouTube* users helped the clip amass over 11 million views.

Horror struck Colorado right before the London Games. On July 20, a gunman entered the midnight screening of *The Dark Knight Rises* at Century 16 Theatres in Aurora. Twelve lives were taken, and 58 people were injured.

Missy found out about the tragedy while she browsed *Twitter* and found her high school's city trending. A good friend had intended to see the movie's first showing. For several hours, the swimmer was terrified, awaiting news of her friend's fate. Thankfully, she finally discovered that he was safe, having chosen to see the film at a different theater.

Not surprisingly the media contacted Missy for her thoughts about the shooting. Devastated for all affected, she vowed to swim in the memory of the victims.

"Every single race I'm going to have that in the back of my mind," she said. "Hopefully, I can make Colorado proud and bring a little bit of light there."

On the morning of July 27, Missy's Olympic competition officially began. The phenomenal athlete would be America's first female swimmer to compete in seven events. In addition to four individual events, she would swim in three relays.

When Missy arrived at the Aquatics Centre on the swimming competition's first day, screaming fans packed the stands. She smiled excitedly while marching to her start position with teammates Jessica Hardy, Lia Neal and Allison Schmitt for the 4×100-meter freestyle relay. At the event's conclusion, she owned her first Olympic medal, a bronze.

"Relays are so important to me," she stressed. "And so important to USA Swimming. We love them and we have so much fun with them."

Two days later, Missy tackled her first individual competition, the 100-meter backstroke. The anxious swimmer sat in the Ready Room with the other competitors. Fifteen minutes earlier she had swam in the 200-meter freestyle semifinals. Could she summon the energy for the next race?

"In lane five, the winner of gold in the 200-meter backstroke at the 2011 FINA World Championships, representing the United States of America, Missy Franklin!"

The 17-year-old waved to the crowd en route to her starting position. Supportive friends, family and fans swayed American flags. Missy waited by the pool. As swimming enthusiasts cheered excitedly, the reality of the moment hit her and she broke into a wide grin.

Seconds later she hopped into the pool and waited for the start signal. Finally, she was off! For much of the race, Australia's Emily Seebohm led the pack. But with less than 25 meters remaining, Missy charged ahead with amazing

"Call Me Maybe"

gusto. When the teen touched the wall with a score of 58.33, she scanned the scoreboard for the final standings. Upon seeing her name in first place, Missy broke into a jubilant smile. Second-place finisher Emily Seebohm and bronze medalist Aya Terakawa from Japan swam over and congratulated her with a hug.

"I am so happy," she gushed. "I knew that tonight was definitely going to be difficult, with that double, but I had a blast tonight."

Later Missy stepped onto the top step of the podium. She grinned ecstatically when an official placed a gold medal around her neck. "The Star-Spangled Banner" blared proudly over the sound system as the American flag soared high above the pool.

"Seeing that flag being raised — all the things that I've gone through passed through my mind…" Missy recalled. "The early morning wake ups, the practices, all the meets… Just all the things leading up to that moment… It was so incredibly worth it."

During the ceremony, the moved gold medalist suddenly glanced at the arena's big screen. For a few seconds the camera rested on her proud parents. Missy's bottom lip quivered as tears clouded her eyes. She tried singing along to her country's national anthem but overwhelming emotions caused her to temporarily forget the lyrics.

"I was trying to sing, I was crying at the same time, I forgot the words, I didn't know what I was doing, I was a huge mess," she later laughed.

Meanwhile her central support team watched with deep emotion. Todd became misty-eyed, and her parents wept, too. In fact, Dick's tears marked his first in 17 years. He last cried on the day his daughter entered the world.

After the event a giddy Missy attended the post-meet press conference. The 17-year-old modeled her medal for photographers. Grinning widely, she slipped the hardware over her head and then giggled.

"Isn't it pretty?" she asked.

As if her dream day couldn't get any better, the swimmer later logged on to *Twitter* to find a special treat.

"Heard @FranklinMissy is a fan of mine. Now I'm a fan of hers too. CONGRATS on winning GOLD! #muchlove," wrote Justin Bieber.

"I just died!" the ecstatic fan tweeted back to the music superstar. "Thank you!"

Golden Girl
(The Associated Press / Lee Jin-man)

The next day the teen placed fourth in the 200-meter freestyle, missing the bronze medal by less than one one-hundredth of a second. Nevertheless the gracious competitor felt elated that her teammate Allison Schmitt took gold in a remarkable record-setting performance.

Even better, Missy reunited with her parents for several minutes that day. The close threesome hugged tightly before the Olympic champion showed her folks her gold medal. When their reunion came to an end, D.A. nervously watched the teen place the medal safely back into her pocket, where she'd been keeping it.

"Make sure your pocket is zipped," Missy's mom cautioned anxiously.

"The mother part of me wanted to take it and put it in my bag and take it back to the house because she's going to lose it," the protective parent admitted to *USA Today.*

Next the focused athlete and Allison regrouped for the 4x200-meter freestyle relay. The two girls walked confidently onto the deck alongside their teammates Dana Vollmer and Shannon Vreeland. The fierce foursome didn't just hope to take first place; they vowed to win in dominating fashion.

As the leadoff swimmer, Missy got the Americans off to a solid start, while Dana and Shannon continued a strong relay. Moments later Allison unleashed a blistering anchor performance that propelled the Americans to gold!

Later Missy and her three teammates proudly stood atop the podium. The giddy athletes inspected their new souvenirs before placing their hands over their hearts while their country's anthem played. Later they grasped hands and raised their arms in triumph. Sharing a gold medal with friends felt incredibly satisfying.

Olympic Bronze
(Getty Images)

Despite the huge victory, though, Missy quickly pushed the thrilling win from her mind. Three events remained on her schedule. She couldn't lose focus. Extended revelries would happen later.

"I know after everything's over, this whole team is going to have a huge celebration and we're all going to be so happy for each other," she remarked. "That's when we can all sit back and appreciate everything we've accomplished as a team."

The next day Missy competed in the 100-meter freestyle. Since it wasn't her strongest event, the swimmer didn't harbor enormous medal hopes. She would up placing a respectable fifth.

"I was just a little bit off my best time and I gave it everything I had so I'm really happy," the competitor remarked.

Throughout the games, Missy's dancing became a frequent conversation topic. Prior to each race, the happy-go-lucky swimmer danced on deck, bopping her body along to the sound system's musical selections. Her carefree nature further endeared her to sports fans.

"Dancing helps me relax so much," she laughed. "Being able to be loosey-goosey and have fun... Dancing is so much fun. It's when I can relax. Bust a move and I'll be set."

The 200-meter backstroke marked Missy's next competition. The strong favorite looked forward to her fourth and final individual competition.

"You know what? I have a lot of confidence in it," she stated. "It's my favorite race. I have so much fun with it, and that's the most important part of it. I love the fact that it's my only event (Friday) and I think that's going to help a lot."

In the end Missy raced a strong, smooth race. By the final stretch she was a full body length ahead of her nearest competitor! The exuberant swimmer broke into a huge smile upon learning she won another gold medal.

"I can't believe what just happened," Missy smiled. "In that last 25, I was giving it everything I had because I couldn't feel my arms and legs and I was just trying to get my hand to the wall as fast I could."

Despite winning a second individual gold medal, the perennial team player also expressed delight that she would share the podium with her teammate, Elizabeth Beisel. Meanwhile Russia's Anastasia Zueva took silver.

Pretty Little Liars
(ABC Family)

Superstar
(PRN / PRPhotos.com)

With Carly Rae Jepsen and Mardy Fish
(Marco Sagliocco / PR Photos)

London Athletes at the 2013 Golden Globes
(Getty Images)

"It feels amazing," she gushed. "It feels so great to have Beiselup on the podium with me. It was so special."

One event remained. Missy could collect a fourth gold medal as part of the United States' 4x100-meter medley team. She would swim the backstroke leg.

Missy kicked off the medley with a strong swim. Rebecca Soni maintained the lead in the breaststroke, and Dana Vollmer proved steady in the butterfly. Finally Allison Schmitt brought the gold home with the freestyle. The team completed the race with a score of 3:52.05, a new world record. They excited competitors shared a group hug, celebrating the historic moment.

Missy's fourth victory matched Amy Van Dyken's earlier record for most gold medals won by an American woman.

With her competitions finished, the young swimmer could finally reflect on her Olympic experience.

"I exceeded expectations," Missy told *The Denver Post*. "I could never have imagined walking into this meet and walking away how I have. I have had so much fun here. I wasn't really expecting gold or world records. I was expecting to get close to my team."

On August 12, Missy Franklin and the American delegation marched into Olympic Stadium to bid farewell to the London Games. The Colorado teen spent the night celebrating and taking pictures with friends, as Annie Lennox, George Michael, The Who and The Spice Girls provided the night's entertainment.

"I am so excited," Missy gushed to *The Associated Press*. "It is the perfect way to end the entire journey."

Near the ceremony's finale, London's mayor Boris Johnson passed the Olympic Flag to Jacques Rogge, the mayor of Rio de Janeiro. The countdown to Rio had officially begun.

First, though, Missy savored the present. She would forever cherish her London memories.

"I've had the time of my life," she smiled. "I've never been happier."

At the VMAs
(David Gabber / PR Photos)

"Water's in my veins."

Chapter 7

SWIMMING SENSATION

Missy entered the 2012 Olympics as a medal contender and left London as a superstar. The teen embarked on a flurry of activities after returning to the United States. Missy Mania had invaded the country! She made several high-profile appearances, including attending the *2012 MTV Video Music Awards* and chatting up Jay Leno.

Missy told very few people her plane's arrival time in Colorado. The humble athlete didn't want to create a big spectacle. Word of her imminent arrival spread quickly, though. When the teen landed at Denver International Airport, a huge crowd welcomed their hometown hero with balloons, American flags and banners.

"It was so awesome," she told *The Tonight Show*. "Their support has been incredible. I wouldn't be where I am today without them."

Despite becoming a household name, Missy still carried normal teenage responsibilities. Just a few days following the Olympics, the high school senior returned to Regis Jesuit for classes. She carried a full load: Forensics Science, Advanced Dance, Economics, Philosophy and AP Literature and Composition.

Less than three months after London, Missy looked forward to a relaxing Halloween. The fun-natured girl always liked handing out candy to trick-or-treaters. When the sun finally set, a parade of costumed children walked through the Franklin's neighborhood. One of the most popular costumes that holiday? Missy Franklin! So many times the Olympic champion would open her front door and be greeted by a miniature version of herself. Needless to say, the tributes tickled her!

About three months later, Missy also had the opportunity to dress up, too, when she secured an invitation to the 2013 Golden Globe Awards. The Olympian enjoyed a fairy tale night as she brushed elbows with Hollywood's biggest actors. Among her famous celebrity encounters: George Clooney, Ben Affleck, Leonardo DiCaprio, Anne Hathaway and Robert Pattinson.

Though her trophy shelf now included Olympic treasures, the teen still took great pride competing on Regis Jesuit's swim team. On February 9, the popular champion led her teammates to a second state title. Upon seeing the official result posted, Missy and her team jumped gleefully into the pool. The unbridled enthusiasm marked a perfect way to end the respected athlete's high school career.

"Just being with my girls in that last moment and crying and knowing it would be the last time I was going to swim with all of them and have a Regis cap on my head. That's why I did it," the respected athlete remarked.

"In 10 years, we'll look back and say Missy Franklin swam for our team for four years and took us to two championships," raved Raiders coach Nick Frasersmith. "It's hard to swallow, almost surreal."

The next month Missy guest-starred on television's *Pretty Little Liars*. The athlete portrayed herself on the popular teen drama. She loved the entire experience.

"Everyone here is so nice and sweet," Missy smiled. "They made me feel so comfortable and relaxed. I had a great time."

"She is amazing," the show's star Shay Mitchell gushed. "I was like, 'Have you done this before?' She is such a natural. She never missed her mark once and remembered her lines."

A champion swimmer, a high school honors student and a talented actress. Was there anything Missy Franklin couldn't do?

"I am a terrible artist," she laughed. "I can't draw to save my life."

Meanwhile sports fans hoping for a glimpse into a elite swimmer's life were thrilled to learn about an upcoming documentary entitled *Touch the Wall*. Armed with over three years of footage, filmmakers Grant Barbeito and Christo Brock chronicled Missy and teammate Kara Lynn Joyce's Olympic pursuit.

Much hoopla centered on Missy's decision to spurn professional opportunities, so she could compete in the NCAA. As her high school graduation approached, college recruiters and sports fans wondered which university she would attend. The much sought-after senior visited several campuses, including University of Georgia, USC and University of Texas at Austin.

In the end, though, one college particularly appealed to her. From the second the swimmer got off the plane and walked on Northern California soil, she felt instantly at home.

"I've committed to Cal Berkley," she finally announced. "There are so many reasons why I chose Cal. The coach is amazing. The team is amazing. I absolutely love it."

There was something else Missy couldn't turn down. The chance to meet Justin Bieber! When the singer flew to Denver for a major concert, he invited his biggest fan backstage for a special tour. He spent several minutes chatting with the athlete and even showed her how to ride a Segway.

"He is truly a wonderful and genuine person," she tweeted. "Such an honor to meet him!"

When Missy wasn't hobnobbing with celebrities, relaxing at home with her folks or on Regis Jesuit's campus, one could always find her at her favorite place, the swimming pool. Rio constantly lurked in the back of her mind. She would be 21 in 2016, an age that many swimming experts consider a prime age for competition.

No matter what happens in Rio or anywhere else… Despite all the awards she accumulates… Missy Franklin will always remain the same down-to-earth girl that charms the world. After all, when all is said and done, the humble athlete doesn't see herself as a superstar. She still considers herself just a teenager who gets to do what she loves every day.

"I still see myself as a girl that just gets to go swim every day with all of her friends," Missy smiled.

Essential Links

Missy's Official Twitter Account
www.twitter.com/FranklinMissy

USA Swimming
http://www.usaswimming.org

Team USA
www.teamusa.org

Missy Franklin Fan Page
http://missy-franklin.com

Missy Franklin Fan Page
http://missyfranklin.com

Touch the Wall Official Site
http://www.touchthewall.com

Rio 2016 Official Site
http://www.rio2016.com

Colorado Stars Online
http://www.coloradostars.org

The Denver Post
www.denverpost.com

University of California, Berkeley
www.berkeley.edu

Todd Schmitz's Official Twitter Account
www.twitter.com/starstodd

Missy's Favorites

Favorite Movie
The Sound of Music

Favorite Food
Mom's Mac n Cheese

Favorite Athlete
Natalie Coughlin

Favorite School Subject
Chemistry

Favorite Singer
Taylor Swift & Justin Bieber

Favorite Color
Pink

Favorite Swimming Event
200-Meter Backstroke

Favorite Sports Team
Denver Broncos

Favorite Hobby
Dancing

Favorite TV Show
CSI: Miami

About the Author

Christine Dzidrums holds a bachelor's degree in Theater Arts from California State University, Fullerton. She has written biographies on many inspiring women: Joannie Rochette, Yuna Kim, Shawn Johnson, Nastia Liukin, The Fierce Five, Gabby Douglas, Sutton Foster, Kelly Clarkson, Idina Menzel and Missy Franklin.

Christine's first novel, *Cutters Don't Cry*, won a Moonbeam Children's Book Award, as did her biography on Miss Douglas. She wrote the tween book *Fair Youth* and the beginning reader books, *Timmy and the Baseball Birthday Party*, *Timmy Adopts a Girl Dog*, *Future Presidents Club* and *Princess Dessabelle Makes a Friend*.

Build Your SkateStars™
Collection Today!

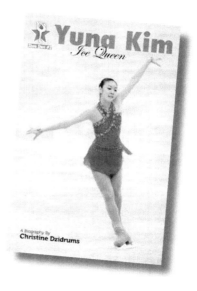

At the 2010 Vancouver Olympics, tragic circumstances thrust **Joannie Rochette** into the spotlight when her mother died two days before the ladies short program. Joannie then captured hearts everywhere by courageously skating two moving programs to win the Olympic bronze medal. *Joannie Rochette: Canadian Ice Princess* profiles the popular figure skater's moving journey.

Meet figure skating's biggest star: **Yuna Kim**. The Korean trailblazer produced two legendary performances at the 2010 Vancouver Olympic Games to win the gold medal. *Yuna Kim: Ice Queen* uncovers the compelling story of how the beloved figure skater overcame poor training conditions, various injuries and numerous other obstacles to become world and Olympic champion.

Shawn Johnson, the young woman from Des Moines, Iowa, captivated the world at the 2008 Beijing Olympics when she snagged a gold medal on the balance beam.

Shawn Johnson: Gymnastics' Golden Girl, the first volume in the **GymnStars** series, chronicles the life and career of one of sports' most beloved athletes.

Widely considered America's greatest gymnast ever, **Nastia Liukin** has inspired an entire generation with her brilliant technique, remarkable sportsmanship and unparalleled artistry.

A children's biography, *Nastia Liukin: Ballerina of Gymnastics* traces the Olympic all-around champion's ascent from gifted child prodigy to queen of her sport.

Also From

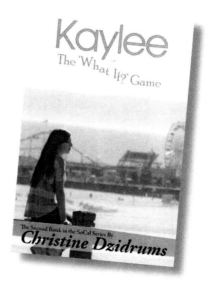

2010 Moonbeam Children's Book Award Winner! In a series of raw journal entries written to her absentee father, a teenager chronicles her penchant for self-harm, a serious struggle with depression and an inability to vocally express her feelings.

"I play the 'What If?'" game all the time. It's a cruel, wicked game."

When free spirit Kaylee suffers a devastating loss, her personality turns dark as she struggles with depression and unresolved anger. Can Kaylee repair her broken spirit, or will she remain a changed person?

Meet **Princess Dessabelle**, a spoiled, lonely princess with a quick temper. When she orders a kind classmate to be her friend, she learns the true meaning of friendship.

Build Your Timmy™
Collection Today!

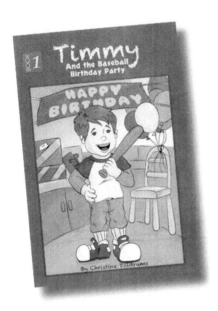

Meet Timmy Martin, the world's biggest baseball fan.

One day the young boy gets invited to his cousin's birthday party. Only it's not just any old birthday party... It's a baseball birthday party!

Timmy and the Baseball Birthday Party is the first book in a series of stories featuring the world's most curious little boy!

Timmy Martin has always wanted a dog. Imagine his excitement when his mom and dad let him adopt a pet from the animal shelter. Will Timmy find the perfect dog? And will his new pet know how to play baseball?

Timmy Adopts A Girl Dog is the second story in the series about the world's most curious 4½ year old.

Twelve-year-old Emylee Markette feels invisible. Then one fateful afternoon, three beautiful sisters arrive in her sleepy New England town and instantly become the most popular girls at Forest Springs Middle School. To everyone's surprise, the Fay sisters befriend Emylee and welcome her into their close-knit circle.

Through it all, though, Emylee's weighed down by nagging suspicions. Why were the Fay sisters so anxious to befriend her? How do they know some of her inner thoughts? What do they truly want from her?

When Emylee eventually discovers that her new friends are secretly fairies, she finds her life turned upside down yet again and must make some life-changing decisions.

Fair Youth: Emylee of Forest Springs is the first book in an exciting new series for tweens!

Ashley's favorites

1. Favorite movie — under dog

2. Fav food — Mac and Cheese

9. Fav tv Show — Dog with a Blog

3. fav athlete — Missy Franklin & Micheal Phelps

4. fav school subject — Recess

5. fav singer — Katy perry & Tay swift

6. fav color — Green

7. Fav swim event — 50 breastroke

CPSIA information can be obtained at www.ICGtesting.com
Printed in the USA
BVOW01s0041090514

353019BV00012B/393/P

8. Fav hobby — being active